# TURNING TO FICTION

# TURNING TO FICTION

*Poems*

## Donna Masini

W. W. NORTON & COMPANY

NEW YORK LONDON

Copyright © 2004 by Donna Masini

Book design by Lovedog Studio
Production manager: Julia Druskin and Andy Marasia

Library of Congress Cataloging-in-Publication Data

W. W. Norton & Company, Inc.
500 Fifth Avenue, New York, N.Y. 10110
www.wwnorton.com

W. W. Norton & Company Ltd.
Castle House, 75/76 Wells Street, London W1T 3QT

1 2 3 4 5 6 7 8 9 0

ISBN 978-0393-32844-8

*For my mother and father*
*with love and gratitude*


*and in memory of Sarah Wells, June Jordan,*
*Michael Maggiar, and Sarah Pettit*

# Contents

## II.

## III.

Some of these poems first appeared in *American Poetry Review*, *Tri-Quarterly*, *Open City*, *Lyric*, *Pequod*, *The KGB Bar Book of Poems*, *Washington Square*, and *Bleecker Street II*.

For many kinds of sustenance and support, for their imagination and generosity, I am grateful to Marie Howe, Jan Heller Levi, Rita Gabis, Mark Doty, Judd Tully, Tony Hoagland, Victoria Redel, Honor Moore, Daniel Mendelsohn, Michael Massing, Walter Mosley, Ghislaine Boulanger, Carol Conroy, James Conrad, Medrie MacPhee, Jeff Rindler, Christopher Berger, Michael Marco, David Cohen, Carlos Moore, Nancy Anderson, Eve Grubin, Karen Backus, and my editor, Jill Bialosky.

I am grateful to the Corporation of Yaddo and the National Endowment for the Arts.

He kindled your desire and bound you to him
by a chain of such longing. . . .

*The Cloud of Unknowing*


**Fill in the blanks:**

1. Before entering the confessional box we
   should try especially to arouse in our
   hearts_____

*The Baltimore Catechism*

# I

# A Sign

*Think About Sex*, the billboard says.
Red letters above the empty
restaurant, the tarot stand with its vague

promises. I am
thinking about sex, about the way we
sleep—desire thrumming, the air

thick with it, without coming
across the borders of our yearning.
Without touching. The man above us

bangs in: 5 a.m., knocking across the floor
with his various companions.
Last night before sleeping we fingered

reproductions of Sienese Madonnas, their falling
half-open books, wrinkled babies.
Annunciations, the grave

faces of women who would conceive,
birth a child without pleasure, without sex,
in humility not thinking, gazing out across centuries

with their stony features as if each visitation announced
the birth of holiness, purity, God
I am thinking about sex, days shaped by desire

the way those paintings are shaped
by a chain of radiance, a gold trembling
light. What draws this man

into my bed? What propels me—what love
of desire, refusal—to watch him lean into others,
pressing, remembering

the way he touched me, the promise.
I am thinking about sex (I've always been obedient)
and it seems just now there are two kinds of love:

love that is returned and love that is not
physical, though returned in spirit, pure
hell—two souls knocking against one another,

the steady drill of them, like the misguided
dragonfly driving into the brick
wall under this billboard. I am thinking about sex,

about desire, the way I wait for a sign,
a half-open book, wanting
something to reveal
what all this longing longs for.

# Two Grapefruits

My husband made me juice—
each morning rose and in the kitchen,
in the early light idling through blue glass,
crushed the fruit, palmed it across
the juicer, filtered the pits and pulp and
carried it back to me, rubbing my shoulder
as I drank. My lover
rises early—hours before me—
slices the fruit and with a curved, serrated
knife, dissects each section, carefully separating
the membranes, as they say God first sliced
the person in two—man and woman—so that
each would ache for its other.
I want them both. I want the juice and the meat,
that pure exquisite liquid and the tender
flesh, the reddish pulp. All of it.
If you get the pure juice, you lose
the juicy flesh and if you eat the flesh you miss
the way the juice goes down. So easily.

# Three Card Monte

They're at it again. On Broadway, the crowd
closes around the dealer, his cards facedown in the uncertain
sun. They never win, but they keep

coming back. Last night I slept with him again.
Again the long sexless night. What sends them
back, what makes them

inch up, into his chants, throwing their burning hard-
earned cash, what propels them
to that table? Is it his beautiful hands, the voice
    that makes him

luster? It looks easy. They're sure to win.
They must. They can see the trick, the sly
card they have outwitted. Behind them the Tower

Record sign, the cheap eager dresses on racks, the Broadway
    traffic.
Again and again I go back to him, banging against him,
certain this time, this time . . .

Who would have thought love would come so slowly.
December it seemed a sure thing. I raced into it,
announced myself, the way I've read salmon

leap against a stream,
that awful arc, the way music will build, ache, but release
doesn't come. *I love you,*

he says. Month after
month I fall for it, fill up with it,
ticking down Broadway, the way those salmon—how do
    they?—

stupid, lusting, plunging. The crowd scatters
its disappointment, each trying to figure
how he'd lost, it had really looked like,

she'd been certain, it had seemed so certain,
those beautiful hands, that voice, and now
a new crowd begins to form. Face after stupid face.

# Natural History

For lack of a better direction I steered us
into the *Biology of Invertebrates*. We watched
the way the spineless milky creatures grew

luminous at night. Jellyfish hung—glassy, diaphanous.
A bluish squid pinned to the ceiling itching
to squander its inky diffusions.

I wanted to be wowed, knocked out.
I wanted to place us somewhere
unchangeable. We stood at the diorama—

static, dramatic. A soft wind blew
the sea grass like a deep-sea car wash,
anemones spread their delicate tentacles, swaying

among jumbled clusters of silver fins—a stupor
of spawning. Above it a parrot fish slept, suspended
in its gelatinous sac. Everything in its place.

There was a space (labeled *angelfish* in the key below).
Whatever had been there must have fallen
among the soft corals that

reach by night their wavering tentacles

capturing whatever happens

to drift through their chambers—

# Slowly

I watched a snake once, swallow a rabbit.
Fourth grade, the reptile zoo
the rabbit stiff, nose in, bits of litter stuck to its fur,

its head clenched in the wide
jaws of the snake, the snake
sucking it down its long throat.

All throat that snake—I couldn't tell
where the throat ended, the body
began. I remember the glass

case, the way that snake
took its time (all the girls, groaning, shrieking
but weren't we amazed, fascinated,

saying we couldn't look, but looking, weren't we
held there, weren't we
imagining—what were we imagining?)

Mrs. Peterson urged us to *move on girls*,
but we couldn't move. It was like
watching a fern unfurl, a minute

hand move across a clock. I didn't know why
the snake didn't choke, the rabbit never
moved, how the jaws kept opening

wider, sucking it down, just so
I am taking this in, slowly,
taking it into my body:

this grief. How slow
the body is to realize.
You are never coming back.

# Summer

Cold for July. The fire won't start.
The logs, damp in their crib, won't ignite.
I crumple paper, light it, toss kindling into the pot-
belly stove. The ends catch, curl and the flame
goes out. Ashes smolder in the grate.
Termites labor in the table legs. The screen doesn't fit,
rattles in its jamb. My book lies
unread on the table, the weight of blood
heavy in me, and finally I can recover
those seven weeks it lived in me,
doubling, turning
my urine bright. The ceiling
fell in chunks, pigeons fucked
behind the window, and I was afraid
of small things: an envelope, an afternoon.
I measured my grief the way you measure
a room for furniture. Too much
happened in that room. A mirror
blocked my window so I saw myself
when I looked out and couldn't see what I imagined
was an air shaft, ticking with pigeons,
their ecstatic scramble, knocking the glasses, the canisters
of tea on the shelf. I was surprised by the violent
knock of body to pane, the force of what
I knew but could not see.

## This Girl's Mother Kept Her Umbilical Cord in a Glass Jar on the Top Shelf of the Kitchen Cabinet

(Later the girl would be afraid
to leave pieces of herself—hair, a clipped-off nail—
in a strange place, even
a tissue she might have used. She
would press herself into strangers
as if they were houses,
house herself against the basement wall,
brick stoop, shed, side of an elevator, even once a rock.
She'd tongue salt off the skin of rough-necked men—
an odd habit, an agitation.
She wanted to build herself
into someone else.)

# Communion

We called it "receiving," and each of us in our bridal
white, walked down the aisle toward the Body
of Christ, our poofy dresses and veils floating, crowns

on our heads, clutching our rosaries and bouquets—those
carnations we'd lifted out of green tissue from the florist's
    box.
(Does any flower have a fresher smell?) I led the procession

with Kathy Creamer, rows and rows of tiny brides.
We had not eaten. We had not drunk. We had confessed
the day before. We were pure. We would never be so pure
    again

once the body had entered us. We made our way back
down the aisle. I held the disk my body
had prepared itself to carry, lightly on my tongue, careful

not to let my teeth graze the host. I know I smiled an idiotic,
    beatific smile.
Later I'd say it was because I was receiving
the Lord (I'd bow my head and say the name) *Jesus*,

but even then I knew I was acting, faking it, my spirit rising
above that aisle—looking down on the rows of us to see how
    I looked
now I had received. Maybe that's why, back in our pews, we
    were told

to put our heads in our hands—to keep us from drifting.
To keep us in our bodies. We knelt, face in hand, and
    waited.
Or maybe it was too much to see that very man—the
    Incarnation

stretched before us—naked but for the floating cloth—
those beautiful legs stretched across the altar and we girls,
    having received,
kneeling under the groin vault. Or maybe we just couldn't

let anyone see our faces when finally, after years of waiting,
we held it in our mouths—Corpus Christi—that first time,
that first man we took into our bodies.

# The World Gains Luster as It Falls Apart

Nothing but light, nothing
       but glitter nearly obliterating the shape you make
          on the icy beach, nothing

but the way you
       squint into the light, the lens, at whoever
          is taking this picture that arrests me. (What

made you send this?) I know
       the caution in that smile. You're lost
          in the dazzle

of sand and light, your
       arm raised, hand poised
          as though you are holding out

a tiny shell but I know there's nothing
       there, just the way your arm moves
          out when you're cold

as if to indicate the cold
       were to feel it
          less. As if you were trying

to let the icy air down
       your arm and out your fingertips. Maybe
              it's the cold, the way the sun splinters

the picture that makes me think
       of last winter, after the blizzard, the way we
       walked across Brooklyn,

minced and edged
       over the Brooklyn Bridge.
           I'd felt trapped in our dark

apartment, wanted
       the glitter, the city.
           Days we'd been stuck, the snow

constricting. In the blinding
       ice I see us, holding
           one another. Why didn't we stay home?

*Treacherous*, you said. I didn't think
       we'd make it. My fingers burned and
       I had no idea where we were

going, just that we were
       trying not to fall, not to slide.
           I'd never walked on ice like that

and I've said nothing
        about the wind. Though we were moving
                forward all the time, it looked the same

from any place. A kind of icy stasis.
        We slid, I almost fell, it was like nothing
                we'd ever done. The sun

made bars across the ice,
        a lonely moaning wind.
                The city had never

glittered like that
        and we kept feeling
                our way into that glitter.

# Longing

Once we were together
I missed just sitting beside him, in a crowded
room, say, his sleeve rolled
just below the elbow, the muscle
swelling. It was promise, it was Catherine and
Heathcliff, the phone call that might
come. Then it was just another part of him.
Just an arm. But just
now I thought of him, I thought yes, the arm.
*His* arm. His *arm*.
Now that it's over it is luminous again.

## Phone Sex

She's lying
on her bed, she tells him—

in fact
she's on the floor,

a chair, who knows—isn't this
desire, the naked offering

across the city—a virtual
net of confession, a ritual

stickiness of longing and static.
He asks her to lie

down, blindfold herself, touch
her breasts—one, then the other,

finger the nipples. Now get a belt.
It's touching really

what one stranger will do
for another. He tells her

he will gag her. This
is what she's wanted. A man

who will listen
to what she cannot whisper in the dark,

on a couch, bed, desktop, chair, kitchen table, hell
even her office floor where she breathes

quietly after fingering herself.
She's wearing (you choose):

black lace, white silk, T-shirt, hiked skirt, jeans
unzipped. She wipes

sweat from her damp
hair. It's what he wants—to pillage

the soft
country between her thighs,

as if she were a walled
city and he, the conquering hero.

But she's admitted
him, she's pressed the button

to indicate she is ready
to connect, live, now

they're voice to voice,
tongue to tongue, pumping

the manic narrative, the provincial
emergency of desire. Imagine

what drives them, room to room.

# What She Can't Say When He Leans Toward Her and Whispers *Begin*

She wants a lock on her door, things
      like that—small things. She is afraid
            of large spaces, the new development—the way

whiskey smells when she walks past
      the bar, her school bag scraping.
            And she loves the drift

of men's voices, though she runs quickly past.
      She's always holding her foot against a door.
            (*But it is only someone knocking.*)

There was a man at the basement door, white hair,
      bristles on his chin. He looked strangely
            like a baby. *Will* his name was—

or *Mr. Will*—peeking through
      the glass. This man in the snow (she saw him)
            peeling an orange, tearing

the white shreds from the fruit,
      the way children and the anxious pick at their lips.
            In the basement (the concrete walls covered

with blue paint, the floor cold, the dryer tumbling
    it's wrung-out lives) her father turns
        into himself, moves among the burners, the
        boilers, the heat.

She hides there reading *The Diary of Anne Frank.*
    He tries to start the barbecue *inside* (it is raining).
        How many lives tumbling in the terrible pages.

She holds these things, what she can't
    fit into a sin, never, in the dark box, her divided,
        her most grievous heart, confess.

It is like
    carrying a full glass of
        water up the stairs, ready to

spill. Everything
    moves. Everything
        is moving.

Now the priest leans toward the screen.
    She will always love listening to men
        whisper in the dark. Waiting for absolution

she kneels in the box the way she
    crouches in her closet, filling up
        with a radiant agitation. Or is it joy?

It surprises her, filling up like this.
    She shivers with it, pressed to the screen,
        a latched girl flickering.

# Ending

The wild sigh of
pigeons in the air

shaft, how they cry
and cry after their spectacular

flutter and rise,
the men breaking down

something in back
of this building, the heat

rattling, climbing
in its pipes, the teakettle,

its high mourning
sigh—hard to believe it's just

water. The noon
siren, the lone cat shrieking for its

tom, and that child
two flights up. What is this

cry in the pipes?
This hissing steam?

This thin whistle of sorrow?

# Persuasion

We are at the *Paris*, watching
the heroine struggle in our plush seats, the screen
enormous before us the way screens were

when we were kids and stars seemed
larger, not like now when they feel
so small you could put several

in your mouth and swallow them.
I wish Jane Austen had created me,
I lean into Carol and whisper

and almost miss a scene,
a crucial decision on the heroine's part
which wouldn't be the first

crucial decision I've missed.
That slow exquisite thinking that allows
the self to light itself up,

a Venetian glass candleholder
seen from *inside*. All year I've been watching
myself flicker, unsure

whether I was seeming stronger or
going out, the word *journey*
banging around inside me.

Now it happens
the image splits, the heroine seems
slightly incongruous—a lustrous

double slipping out, a spirit urging
itself across the screen, like fog
blowing off the stars.

**II**

# Girl Reading

Reader, it seemed only natural
that after the difficult
talk, after I wept and walked

in the new dark—I came back, crawled
into bed and turned to fiction,
the way a woman without a home might

shelter in an abandoned building, the way
as a girl I curled around my library
copy of *Jane Eyre*. I was drawn

to small spaces—hallways, crawl space—
I closed myself inside an old washing machine,
squatted in the mirror of my mother's eye.

*What do you expect to see*, the teacher asked,
*in a mirror? What does Jane see?* Jane sees
a monster, doesn't recognize herself

in that small room, locked and punished
by her reflections, flinging herself
on the wretched carpet. What do you do

when the same space you're locked in
you use for hiding? I fell
into reading as a fleeing criminal

moves into a safe house. Alone, shut in,
elbows toughening on the bedspread bumps
while Jane hid in the drapes from John who beat her

with his book. Downstairs my mother
beat the eggs, shook
the rug out the window, always on the verge

of opening the door (Jane was found).
*I can read you like a book. I can see*
*right through you.*

Today the dark came early, took me
by surprise though I'd known it was coming.
All morning winding back

clocks, I put my watch back, the wall
clock, alarm clock, the phone machines
and VCR, all day

the light shrinking, the fall coming.
Then the difficult talk. *Reader,*
*I married him.* Years ago I

borrowed a life. It was a good life,
but a man is not a book and I couldn't see
what held me.

What I expect in the mirror frightens me:
a glass vial, a swarming hive, I am a monster,
Jane says. Damp afternoons doubled over my book

I read in the dark, in the early
morning while the rest of the house
slept. I read in the basement sprawled

across the dryer, the heat ticking, my mother
wheezing. Jane had no mother and Anne's
mother was too close—a few feet away

in that airless attic. *There was no possibility
of taking a walk.* But I had a book
I'd borrowed myself,

chosen among the faded
bindings, the fingered leathers. I imagined
the lives—Jane and Anne,

the readers, years of them, imagined
their bodies, the secret desires that dampened their
fingers, wrote their stories, those girls,

curled in beds around these same books,
what prisons their yearning
had become, what doors.

# Chair

It reminds me of a confessional, the way the screen would
slide and I'd begin, kneeling on my cushion, shut in the
    oak box,

the whisper, my litany of sins. I'm lying
on my bed, on a phone session with my shrink. She's talking
    about dissociation,

the ways I leave myself. I am thinking about this chair my
    husband
and I carried home before the separation, when *husband* was
    a word

that made me feel safe, and the word—*auger* is it?—for the
    tool that makes holes in wood.
In fact (I look it up) it's an *awl* that cuts the wood. You split

yourself, my shrink is saying. I slide the dictionary back in its
    slot,
put my finger to a hole the awl made.

When I was a kid we knelt, my sister and I, on either side of
    the kitchen chair,
and one would be the priest and one would be the sinner.

The sinner would whisper through the chair-back holes, not
   her list of offenses—
*I lied five times, I ate meat on Friday*—sins she might tick off

in a box to the priest, his profile through the screen, hand to
   forehead,
leaning forward, shielding his eyes but looking

as if he had a headache—not lists, but stories: *I watched a*
   *boy*
*peeing behind the Vandeveer projects. That green book with*
   *the picture*

*of Mother Cabrini, my father's pen with the naked lady—I*
   *stole them.*
*I threw out my liverwurst sandwich. I thought about the*
   *starving*

*but Claire Haggerty sat on it at morning Mass.* It was a relief
to tell the whole story now no one was instructing us to keep
   it brief.

The priest doesn't want excuses, Sister Agnes said. He's busy.
He doesn't want to hear about the tear in your dress, how
   beautiful the cake looked

before you stuffed it in your mouth. I am a glutton
he wants to hear. And your contrition. But my sister wanted
    stories

and I would tell them (most of the time I was the sinner).
I'd glory in it, making up plots, characters, dramatic and
    precise

as the punishments Sister Agnes elaborated, ( *for this lie
a girl was struck dumb . . . for showing off her bare arms Our
    Lord turned a girl like yourself*

*into a leper*), specific as hell with its particular
shrieking, its headless burning flesh. My friend Daniel tells
    that joke

about the Woman Taken in Adultery. *Let he who is without
sin,* Jesus says, *cast the first stone.* A huge rock shoots past,

knocks the woman down. Jesus looks up. *Mom,* he says,
*I was trying to make a point.* I love the literal. I loved holding
    the Body

of Christ in my mouth imagining his long legs and forgiving
    smile. I loved
kneeling with my sister at that kitchen chair, peeking, watch-
    ing the pleasure

my story gave. Once, in the confessional, the word *why?* shot
   back through the screen.
Because, I said, my mother forgot it was Friday. She made

pork and beans. God knew, she said, we didn't have money
   to waste.
I had to choose between one sin and my mother, the joke
   would go. I ate the beans.

Now, the priest said, I had my mother's sin, too, on my soul.
   I absolve you,
my sister would say, at the end of my stories. We'd stand,
   knees aching, unable to look

at one another, and spin, as Sister Agnes said God made the
   world spin—quickly—
to keep us still, then we'd fall, panting on the floor, breathing
   in the collaborating dark.

# Reconciliation

There was a line, a screen, a priest who would absolve
you for the thoughts and faults that longing sparked to sin
as if you were a problem he might solve,

an oozing burn, a cut that needed salve
to join the parted skin. For the trouble you were in
there was a line, a screen, a priest who could absolve,

make whole again what passion had dissolved
(like a glass of water that you drop a tablet in
and watch like it's a problem you can solve)

conjoining in solution what was separate, half-
hearted, two parts, good/scarred, broken skin—
no line, no screen, and nothing to absolve.

Divorce is a just a matter of resolve,
to break apart (no fault) what might have been
absolute; you, too, merely a problem to be solved,

a part of the solution you revolve
love, by default, around another, spin
across a line no priest can now absolve,
a problem he might watch but never solve.

# The Trap

I looked away, then back
without my glasses. Only
a blur: dark, furry, shadowed.
I couldn't look. I looked

to where I'd set the trap flush to the space
behind the oven where I'd seen the quick blur run
that afternoon, past the chair, the shelf of books, past
my terror of fur, ancient, dun-colored,

something like a dream that leaves
a mood, an almost-image, that finally gets away.
I saw the stuck fur shudder
to unglue. I sickened and then

left it. I left it
as I have left friends
shuddering in their beds, wheezing among their
birds, their griefs and hypodermics. I couldn't watch

the struggle in the dust, all night
shudder under the shuttered dark. All
night the fur hummed a numb chord. Every noise
was its noise though I'm told they're quiet.

What do we wait for?
I waited for a squeal.
To hear that foul clump of dusty fur
suffer under the oven. I wanted

to love it, its twitching
tail whipping the floor, the air, its heart
a pulsing bomb that would explode
right through its fur, like those cartoon hearts

in cartoon mice. Love made them
thrum, and fear
of love. I have feared love. A furry thing.
It sickened me and so I looked away.

I didn't want to see its little claws hugged up,
the way the back legs twitched,
buried in this dark apartment.

# Half Her Story

She can see it now—her old life
glittering. Nothing
holds. The husband. The lover.
The way he touched her back
between the poetry and fiction
sections at the bookstore, in late summer,
when they were still secret, placed
the delphinium, a small bunch, on her new table,
*all my heart, all my matter*, the shape
the bars made when light came through his window.
Sometimes she thinks it hardly matters at all.
Go ahead, look at her doubled
over there by the subway entrance
heaving, weeping, no longer believing the bright
fish inside her—the heavy minerals
waving, shifting, as everything that flies
rises in her. Only half her story
bleeds through her skin—the rest
whispers in her as she lies
closer to the truth. Once she began
to break down, once
her body began to yield (the body
with all its fluids and shifts, its sucking),
she knew there was no going back,

and she knew she'd lose
everything. Was it greed
that made her want two lives?

# Writing the Story

When I bought that cookbook I was wanting
a warm kitchen, a kitchen light
inside, yellow

the way lights look yellow when you are the person
outside, you
are the person in the dark and someone you imagine

is curled up in a quiet chair, knowing she is loved,
reading a novel, say, *Portrait*
*of a Lady*. Isabel

stands by the piano. Madame Merle
has yet to wreck everything. You don't
fear her yet. You stand in the dark outside

the woman inside is reading. I wanted what she had
and I could make it. See
I've made the kitchen, the chair, the woman.

I've put love into her life, the way as a girl I'd place
bookmarks in other people's books, pencil notes
in the borrowed margins. At closing time

I carried armloads from the library,
stopping to read (I couldn't wait) by the dark
path behind the train trestle, the place

*something* happened. A word
I didn't know. *What do you mean—rape?*
my mother asked when I said my friend

Alice had been raped. They had, the boys had, taken off
her shirt. *No,*
she said, *that's not rape.* She looked strange,

like the time the man from Echo
Caverns (*you are wery nice,* he said—he was Amish)
the man had, well

I've written a story about this. In the story
the girl is nearsighted (I was) reading
a guidebook. Her mother is wearing high heels. The guide

is looking at the mother and the girl (Gina)
is asking questions, trying to get him
to look at *her.* The man puts his arm around her

(me, I mean, he put his arm around me).
We are (were) in Hershey, Pennsylvania, had just toured
the factory, thousands of spinning kisses,

(why call them kisses?) The man squeezed my breast.
*Wery pretty*, he said, but he was looking
at my mother who was repeating

a story about the kisses. Later
we climbed the many stairs—*Tiers*
I say in the story—*like a wedding cake.*

Outside I confessed. *He touched me,*
I said. My mother looked at me—that window
shutting kind of look. I saw my head,

tiny mosquito body in the eye
of her sunglasses and her thinking: why
would anyone touch *her* when *I* was there?

In the story the girl imagines herself
climbing inside the mother's eye, hungry
to be safe inside the story

mother who's holding a cigarette, wearing that
slammed shut look. *She's got some imagination,*
the mother says, lighting up.

# Learning to Read

### 1.

Her mother taught her to read,
"Buh-lack," her mother whispered at the kitchen table,

and slid her red nail along the squiggly letters.
"Duh-og," she said, the red nail moving.

Her mother smelled like roses. Her breath
tickled the girl's neck. "Buh-lack duh-og,"

the girl repeated, her mother
leaning over her. She could feel

the line of shapes form into the running dog.
"Black-dog. Red-house. The-man-walks,"

the girl read. The world moved.
Once her mother gave her a piece of paper, a black crayon.

She spelled the girl's name. She wrote it down. The girl loved
to draw the round *D*. To trace the mother's words. The letters

joined: *banana, mother, umbrella, God.*
But the paper was small. The girl began

to use the wall. *Girl, Mother, Love,* she scrawled.
This was the beginning.


**2.**

Her mother said she could read her like a book,
but her mother didn't read books. She pushed into the girl's
    room
hands up to keep the suds from dripping.

She didn't like it when the girl sat alone doing God
knows what. Her mother had *Gone with the Wind* shoved in
    the junk
drawer among the wedding favors and rubber lids.

The girl imagined her mother separating
her face at the ear, peeling back the skin. She could see her-
    self
layered with pages, the black print across her body.

I can see right through you, her mother said.
The girl lay on her bed, stared at the ceiling. The peeling
layers of paint and cracked plaster. A map

of shapes shrieking between countries.
I can see right through you, her mother repeated. The girl
wondered if it meant she was invisible, transparent, like
    Jell-O,

like the life-sized model of the body in the doctor's waiting
    room,
if her mother could see her heart and veins, the blood run-
    ning through her
like the organs under the plastic page in (she hadn't seen this
    yet) *Gray's Anatomy,*

if she could see her soul, the way you see through your hand
when you hold it above a candle. You're rotten to the core,
    her mother said.
The girl saw thick hot tar running through her. Jesus

pointing to his bloody heart. *Omniscient, omnipotent,*
    *omnipresent,* her book said.
*God sees everything.* The way she peed, cupping her hand
    beneath her,
the hot urine catching in her palm. The way she rolled across
    her blankets,

wrapped her legs around them. She turned onto her stomach.
She didn't feel invisible. She felt like a bag of sand.
I know your tricks, her mother shouted heading back

to the kitchen. I know *all* about you.

### 3.

"You've got quite a stack there," a voice called from behind.
The girl was walking home from the library. A man

stepped out of the trees. Wavy hair, dark eyes.
Like the man on the cover of *The Virgin and the Gypsy*.

He smiled. His teeth
gleamed. The girl would remember a large turquoise ring.

She pushed her hair back, hugged her books, arranged
*The Stranger* at the top of her pile.

It was dark. Without her
glasses the girl could not even see the

stairs to the trestle that crossed the tracks. She wanted
to move, felt she *should* move. "Maybe—" she said.

"Relax," he said. "It's not that," she said, referring to nothing.
"So you got a love story in that pile?" The girl still

did not move. His teeth looked like tiles in an ashtray.
He had taken a handful of her hair. Maybe, she thought,

he was drawn to her, like Birkin to Ursula. Like Heathcliff
to Catherine. "What's your name?" she asked.

She'd never heard of such a name.
"Preston," she repeated. He moved against her, knocked her

books to the ground, grabbed one wrist, moved her other
hand down the front of his pants. The girl felt the word form

inside her. She stared
at the scattered books, thought of her

mother at the sink washing dishes. The foamy suds. The
      carved pumpkin lit
by a candle in the kitchen window. The way the face col-
      lapsed just after

Halloween. She thought of Jesus, the Passion.
Maybe this was passion. Passion is what she'd imagined—

reading, dreaming. The penis moved.
She had forgotten about it. She held her hand over it

lightly, the way you hold your hand over your mouth to quiet
      your breathing.
The man had a smell like chicken soup.

This incident began to fold itself into her, a padding, a layer
for others that would follow. When the girl thought of them

they were shaped like coils in pictures of the brain.

Her own stories. And her mother? Never even saw them.

# Termites

The first night I heard it—a soft whirr,
my friend beside me, gnawing. In the morning
I said I heard you, grinding. And she said,

I heard you, too. You didn't sound so bad,
I said, not like the men we've been with have told us:
like billiard balls hacked with an axe.

No, she said, you either. We agreed. It was delicate—
a serious sound, the way a young girl might
linger over a favorite book. Neither of us said it but I thought

*ladylike*. That day we moved through closets, schoolbooks,
    Father's
Day cards. We tossed out photographs, antique dresses.
It was Memorial Day—my chance to throw away

what I'd tried to save: headboards, marriage, a blue shirt
softened by laundering until its threadbare
cotton arms hung limp. But this was

another couple. I was helping take apart
the house. We were grimy, tired. She boxed. I bagged.
I lifted. She carried. Occasionally she'd hold out

something. A blouse. Out, I'd say, and she'd say,
Yes. No. Ok. No keep it. Usually I agreed.
We were getting rid of things, leaving

the men we couldn't remember
loving us, men who'd made our hearts
shudder. We worked steadily.

That night we slept, a little fitful, the grinding
steadier, slightly—not really louder—
more—insistent.

In the morning I said it was a little—
no, it didn't keep me up, not really, a little
intense. Yes, my friend said, you too.

The third night the grinding, breathing
labored, the way a truck grunts gearing up,
a wrecking ball knocks down a wall. All night

clenched, tense, we jarred each other, racking up
our separate losses. In the morning we rose together, a little
frightened. We couldn't

look at one another, not right away. Don't show me,
she said. Yes. Terrible. We agreed.
We made coffee, tried to laugh.

It *was* like they'd described. Like a project,
a demolition. These griefs
we couldn't speak to.

In the end, in Brooklyn, I'd pulled out,
one after another, the old records—their cardboard sleeves
chewed through. The Beatles' *White Album*, Joni Mitchell's
    *Blue*

face half gone. Wriggling milky things wormed
across the covers. Termites, the exterminator said.
They're going at it years

before you notice, then half
your house is gone. Termites
had eaten through our walls, photographs,

three years of *Natural History* chewed to grit—the spiny
roads roping through them—years crunched to dust.
Weeks now I've been thinking of disintegration,

the way we hold the bewildered
lives in our hands,
let them go.

# Eleven-Headed Female Figure

*(Dogon Statue. Mali. Artist unknown, date unknown)*

How many jaws clench each night?
How many hungers eleven mouths must
hide. Her heads form a small

birdcage on her shoulders. Her short
legs buckle. What does each head hold?
Which holds her fear

of dogs? Where is the memory—
winter afternoon—Siena—the pink
stones, her mother's breast.

In this one her father has gone
out of the house again. What makes him
sleep like that? Such a long sleep,

the vapor of his breath, hissing.
They'd chiseled out a piece of her and poured their tedious
demands, their fears into her. Where does she rest

them, these eleven echoes, where does she lay them
when she makes love? *You're made of stone,*
the man said. *I don't know what I see,*

he said, *in your eyes*. It's a voice
pretending to be tender, but she knows, she knows
the hard bone of that voice, she has it

in one of her heads—like concrete, though concrete
hasn't yet been invented. She'd love to lie
by a river and she'd give

anything to rest that cage. She saw a picture
(which head had she stored it in?), a twittering
bird. She's an exposed nerve,

Medusa with her cage of snakes.
What holds them, these top-heavy
women? What keeps them going, heads

always poking, snooping into quiet afternoons,
when the body would rather just give.
She waits by the phone, but its just that ringing cage.

If you measure, her head takes up half of her. Space
for all those tables and suitcases, what she took
after the divorce. *That* rattling

around in the cage. It's over over over.
Why eleven heads? Wouldn't ten have been enough?
She's always lugged too much around.

When will she rest, watch the spirit vapor
out of her, sing out of her eleven mouths,
weaving in and out the spaces in her

eleven minds? What is the bowl she bears on her head?
How does she wash her hair?
How many teeth? How many shrinks?

When she hungers to fuck does each head shriek
its many warnings? Use your heads. Use your heads.
Can she ever quiet any of it?

# Dickens Village

**1.**

In the beginning, beneath the tree, on rolls of cotton, beside
the Wise Men, a camel, a kneeling lamb, he placed the
 stable
and the first house—a present—he set just to the left

of Bethlehem. Now my father
has built a village: houses, lamps, trees, trains, his village
has outgrown the story, the living

room, no longer fits beneath the tree. He's moved
the Nativity to the coffee table, mixing it up: the manger,
the Christ Child, and Pip, the lamb beside the ashtray.

*Here*, he says, *I made tombstones.* He tells me
how he shaved them, cut and filed, arranged them
on their graves. I am afraid

he has carved names—*our* names (my father is not supersti-
 tious).
I don't look. *Look*, he says,
and just to the right of the skating rink, my father

has made a pond, and added fish (*real* fish) and inns,
and little lamps in front of the houses. My father knows
about houses. The heart, the heat. It's nothing

he could ever say. He flicks a switch. The lights go on. It's
     Christmas in Dickens Village.
The houses lit. The train set to run through its tunnel,
the dead in their places, the night pressing in.


**2.**

How safe inside these stories—
to come out of the snow, kneel at the fire.

The Christmas my marriage was ending
I watched *Little Women* six times, six times went to see

Marmie knock the snow off her boot, enter the house,
the piano sighing, Jo writing in the attic.

My father lifts a girl—Little Nell, she might be. Her foot
has broken off. He props her on the bench. Later he will fix
     her.

A girl I read her story in this same house.
(To have a daughter who reads.)

There is a house inside our house, a town, a village,
safe the way our house never was—

always a glass falling, breaking, always
the spilled milk, the slap, the scream, always someone breaking

into our rooms. Bleak,
it was a bleak house, but here, now

the safe house housed inside the dangerous one,
the way the present lives inside the past, the past,

the present and somewhere
Mrs. Pergola flouring the pan, the painted blue bicycle

in the living room, my grandmother reaching,
hanging the miniature french horns from her tiny tree.


### 3.

A girl is reading *Great Expectations*
in the bedroom she shares with her sister.
She's in high school. Pip's misery *means* something.

Downstairs her father assembles the Nativity
beneath the tree. Later she will sit beside it,
melt tinsel over the colored lights, book on her lap

while the rest of the house sleeps. She'll drift
off, her book falling, upsetting
the shepherd.

        Now a woman knocks

snow off her boot, walks to the fire.
A girl unlaces her skate, brushes the snow
with her fingertips, imagining her life alone.

A stranger comes to town, settles at the inn,
lifts the feather quilt from his bed. What does he long for?
Goose girl loses one of her eggs,

someone pays the baker for bread, the baker's wife
wrapping the warm loaf, the brown paper crackling.
What is a village? Who are these people?

The Watchman swings his lantern.


**4.**

I would like to live in this village, sleep in the amber
lights that go on when my father comes down to watch over
    it.

A child I watched men when I thought they weren't
looking, imagined them

holding me, shutting the lights while I drifted
to sleep. I could not imagine my father

talking to me, like this young
man who shepherds his girls to the church.

I can believe my father has names for them—these figures
rushing past candleshops, though often he would forget my
      name—

or needed several tries before he got it right.
Music drifts across the pond, the skaters

skating to songs that won't be written for a hundred years.
*City sidewalks, busy sidewalks.*

How little we have known one another.
(To have a daughter who reads.)

I've read these books, I tell him—*The Old Curiosity
Shop, A Christmas Carol*. They saved me.

I don't add from what. Instead I say *God . . .*
Then it's quiet. *Sometimes,*

my father says, (and now he doesn't seem like my father. It's
      a voice
I've never heard), *sometimes I switch off*

*the music* (he reaches below the rink, unhooks the sound). *I sit there* (he points to the couch) *and watch*.

The skaters continue. We hear only the sound—
I'm imagining here—of blade to ice.

*I watch them*, he says. *I just watch*.

# III

# What I Have Left

What I thought were birds
    holding in the waves, floating gulls, were,
        a man said later, *moorings*.

Last night moored by the window, the moon
    wide and low, doubled by panes—*two moons*
        I said to no one, I saw two of them—

the real moon and the one I'd imagined—a pale
    green lure at the end of that—
        *jetty*, the man said. The word

held it there. I'd been reading
    *To the Lighthouse*, never seeing all that time
        the lighthouse out there—the steady beam, the
            solid

cups and shawls—the house dissembling
    and Mrs. Ramsay dead in her parenthesis.
        (Sarah, too, died yesterday)

Each time I come back to it—each
    time Mrs. Ramsay dies between those eyebrows
        I feel the world

disperse—a woman dying
    all those years ago and Prue
        in childbirth dead (Sarah surprised us). I woke

to the green light at the end of that—*jetty*.
    I'd lost my place. And did they
        (I always forget) get there? I shivered at the
            thought,

wanted to tiptoe in my slip out
    to the water's edge, watch night settle, the streets
        empty. But I stayed in that house (too often I'm
            afraid).

Why didn't I go out under the two moons?
    Why didn't I sit by the bay waiting
        for morning? Why didn't I visit

Sarah the week we thought it was only hepatitis?
    Book, light, bird, night—solid
        as this blue cup, the yellow bowl I left (*fringed*
            *with joy*)

on my friend's table. Nothing so solid as a cup.
    Mrs. Ramsay knew that. Yesterday
        with diagrams and arrows the paper said—

*The Universe Will Never Be the Same.*

    I read it, I followed the arrows, looked up

        the words and I still don't understand


neutrinos: that collision, that cone-shaped flash—

    weight, air, (missing) mass. Sarah

        would have known. They weren't birds at all—

        they were


buoys, *moorings* dotting the waves.

    How can a person be there

        then not there? How could I speak to her


and then not, not ever,

    owe her a phone call, a coffee? Somewhere

        I read the soul is like a boat. A sentence


spooling out the way

    a beach continues the water and you

        haven't got a clue. What holds us?


This blue cup in my hands. Mrs. Ramsay dead.

    Andrew in a burst of language shattered

        in that war. Sarah dead on her birthday. This

        time

last year, my marriage over, I got lost on Fire Island.
        A man had marked it on the sand: *here*, he said
            *is the marina, here turn*, but later

it all looked the same. Hours lost in it—
        I couldn't speak for fear. I'd never thought to ask
            what a marina was—a clump of boats I thought,

but all those boat clumps looked the same—bay, ocean,
        which was which? I was thinking *this is my life—lost,*
            why had I left my husband, left

to wander in this hot dry sand (my life).
        Hard not to think metaphor. No,
            not metaphor—*punishment*. It *was* hot as hell.

*Here*, he'd said, and it had made sense
        laid out in the sand. But that was last year.
            I got back, he found me. I told the story—

(Sarah in particular loved that one.)
        All that was then and now
            I walk along the dune grass (I have a map)

through what they call *the moors*,
        everything scraping at me—my losses, my broken
            life before me like a bad movie.

Why say *lose* and *loss* when it was me who left?
　　Maybe the hardest thing about losing
　　　　is the succession of metaphors—

a ceiling falls, a boat circles, a way lost.
　　No, the hardest thing is you are alone. Out of context.
　　　　Released. Unmoored. Booted out of paradise.

You keep having dreams of your husband marrying, wake
　　heavy in your bed, unable to move, grateful
　　　　it was a dream. Only a dream, you say—when you
　　　　know

what dreams are. *Solitude*—
　　a word I threw out once. *Only my feet*
　　　　*making the floorboards creak,* someone wrote.

# Waiting for the Subway to St. Vincent's Reading the *Tibetan Book of Living and Dying*

(*Sarah Wells 1950–1998*)

I am reading about impermanence, the way
everything I thought would last—marriage, the elasticity
of skin, the huge can of dry mustard my husband

(*ex*-husband ) bought by accident—is gone. I need to under-
    stand death,
what to say to my friend. I read quickly, turning pages,
cramming, the way I studied for tests, reading to the last

minute, trying to remember, skipping the inessential—like
    this
part about patience, compassion. I read ahead, looking for
the hall of death, the karma, the bardo. I look down the dark

tunnel, wondering, as I do each morning, if she'll be alive
when I get there. I pace, I lean over the tracks, I try
to read, to know what to tell her, but it's taking so long and

now I'm hissing into the dark—*come,* I sort of growl,
*come, goddammit,* my teeth clenched, something
coarse, deliberate, clawing up through me.

*I hate you, God . . . Please . . .* Now
the lights round the tunnel, the train
is approaching and I am hissing

at the conductor in his lonely square of light—
*I hate you. I hate you. I hate you.*

# Blood

I wanted to give blood: my O
positive, universal blood.
I had it in me—something useful, something

that might help, and for the first time,
on line outside the shocked
hospital, the volunteer calling O

positive, O positive, the bodies still
falling in our minds, what we didn't want to see
entering us, I thought of that

man or woman who might, even now, be walking
around, carrying bright pints of my vital
self, an idea I had one day last year,

the person who'd received my blood—perhaps
been saved by it. I'd saved someone
and I wanted to give more

and more—to watch those bright vials fill up,
watch rescue move through me. Where was she,
that woman—let's say she was

a woman—was she, like me, on line
somewhere—universal donor—waiting to give back
what had been given: her—my—O

positive eager American blood thriving in her?
Had she, like me, stood outside
her building, the unimaginable happening, watching

the smoke and behind the smoke
smoke, then nothing
but smoke, a man beside her snapping

photographs of a blank, a memory,
our blood, our O positive—O God—
blood no longer necessary, the only thing

we had to give.

# Summer 2002: Blackout

The lights
arc for a second, then minutes

later go out completely and for the second
time this year I join the roving

groups of confused, the dazed moving
through streets, poking at cell

phones, guarding our minutes, our cells
unready, not fully charged. Some of us

had gotten in late, forgot—things having,
people say, gotten back to normal. Strange

how little time it takes. Not even a year.
First there's something there

outside your window, at the end
of your street, what you see or

don't see when you walk out on an
ordinary day—

But people have been feeling—
some of us—

back to normal. Somewhat. Then a blackout—
we can't see it yet—it's daytime,

brilliant sun. The clocks
say 12:51, but we are afraid

of what will happen later. The future now
darkening, darkness. Around the corner

a woman feels her way through the vegetable
stand, stocking up. Some of us

buy candles, batteries, many of us looking down
at our cells, praying our remaining

dots hold. Three planes
agitate the air. Jets.

We know what it means. Or think we do.
*This is it*, someone jokes. We wave our nervous

flashlight beams. Testing. We don't
need them yet—maybe just to get through

our hallways. The circle of light jerking
around stairwells. The lights

come back—eight hours later—not much
lost—milk, butter—

# Holy Saturday

*(Michael Maggiar 1951–1993)*

Whoever made this painted egg, whoever
blew the slimy promise
through the tiny needle hole,
watched the yolk drip from its shell,
then cleaned and washed,
prepared the dye, whoever hung
this Easter egg from the pole that holds
the IV sacs, placed the cartoon
bunny on the tip, wound
the purple thread around the pole and dangled it
where morphine dangled yesterday, hooked
to a tube, to a needle in my friend's arm,
as I watched the liquid pain
killer drip through him, through hours
of waiting, when only
two days before we'd joked and hung
soy sauce and mustard packs
beside the IV protein sacs, paraded
through the halls; whoever hung this egg
last night, while Michael grew a little worse,
the man in the next bed choked
behind the fading rayon curtain, a nurse
flew in and out and left

the body covered in a sheet, the way you leave
unbaked loaves to let them rise, (this morning
it was gone, that body), whoever you are, thank you.
This morning Michael is a little better. I don't know
what this means. In his voice the thin bloom and diffusion
of breath I will see misting his oxygen mask
one year from now, but for now, thank you,
for the soundless ball game on the monitor dangling
from the ceiling reminding me of nothing,
for the painted egg hanging on its thread.

# St. Augustine's Dog

(*June Jordan 1936–2002*)


It's a dingy shiver of longing
in a cross of red leash,
shrugged up

to a parking meter, and I'm watching it—
inside an unfamiliar Starbucks, waiting
for my ride, notebook open, 7 a.m.—

sort of sniffing around, yearning
for a word, a rub, a scratch.
I want to go to the curb

and pat him but that would be immediate
gratification. I force myself to sit, observe
the way I want to touch him and the way

he reminds me of a dog—St. Augustine's dog—
I saw in a corner of a painting in Venice and picked up
as a postcard (detail) I left one morning

in my friend's box at the hotel desk—"sorry
I missed you" or "morning, I'm at the café," or
"meet you at 11:30—ok?" the kind of note you leave—

mindless, informational—when you know you'll see the per-
    son
maybe even before they get the note, you're not worried.
When I look up a large man in a black suit has

situated himself between me and the dog.
I don't know much about
St. Augustine's dog, save that he

(Augustine) must have, when he lost his beloved
mother? son? (Adeodatus, I think he was called)
turned to him for consolation.

Do all deaths recall the others, all dogs, other dogs?
Now the owner arrives, with his coffee and bagel,
undoes the leash. I can see the lone dog

(detail) in the middle of nothing, looking up at
something we can't see—in the empty
space of the card, something—you follow

his gaze—that's not there.

# Attending

I want too much
to help. There's nothing to do
at the side of the bed, nothing

I can say to change
what has already begun to take place.
To take *her* place. Occasionally

she gets thirsty. *Ice chips!* I cry,
finally useful, I
strain to spoon the chips, sideways, into her

mouth so I don't drip water on her gown.
Today five Buddhists sit at her bed.
Eyes closed, smiling, they look

content, peaceful, as if they are relaxing in the sun
and Sarah dying before them. I am trying
to learn from this. To sit. Detach. No need

to do anything, say anything, but I am thinking
Buddhists are useless. It's an old story:
Mary idle, clinging to Jesus, listening to all that talk.

Jesus, Martha says, I'm doing all the work.
These damn dishes. Get your own jug of wine.
And Jesus says, Martha, Martha.

The story's always confused me.
I've always sided with Martha. Now I struggle
to sit, just watch and just

as I am thinking this I see Sarah's lips,
working around her teeth. She's
moaning. Six visitors and no one

watching. Jesus, I say, she's thirsty.
I get the spoon, a towel, a cup of chips, begin
to slide them, chip by chip,

through her lips, and they relax,
almost smile. All five Buddhists, eyes closed,
sitting. All seven of us, attending.

# Spiritual Awakening

It's the *Denial of Death* that wakes me, *A Hunger
for God* tumbling to the floor, St. *Teresa's Interior Castle,*
    votive candles,

sacred stones, the baker's alarm I use to time my meditations,
and *The Spiritual Exercises of St. Ignatius Loyola,* falling.

Ritual and exercise to my cats is knocking down, night after
    night, my whole
shelf of spiritual reading: *Confessions of St. Augustine, The
    Dark Night of the Soul,*

it's all the same to them. It's a battle. I'm trying
to teach them to wait. Tonight I was reading about waiting,

about quiet and anxiety. *Fear and Trembling* open on my bed.
You do not find dread in the beast, Kierkegaard says. The
    alarm

is beeping. Gina is rubbing against Meister Eckhart,
Smoky is chewing the corner of *The Cloud of Unknowing.*

Smoky and Gina don't care about *The Cloud of Unknowing*.
   They want
to eat. I stumble through the dark, open the refrigerator,

the small light and quiet air moving toward me as I imagine
   light
moved in the old monks praying in their icy cells, as I imagine

grace, radiance, the vocation I've envied without knowing
what the call would sound like. Smoky and Gina

don't understand waiting and delayed gratification
any more than I do. They don't care about distinctions

between the flesh and the spirit. I open
a can of *Triumph Turkey Cuts in Gravy*, fork it into their
   bowls,

close my eyes and listen to them eat, *Waiting for God*
on the floor beside them.

# Body and Soul

Michael leads us to the center of the dance floor
holding Kenny's hand, Kenny is dragging me and I
can't see Marie behind me, gripping my fingers.

The music (is this *music?*) is pumping, like it's coming
from inside, as if our hearts are the speakers,
desire urging through the wiry ventricles.

I am afraid my heart is going
to explode. The string of us strains, a chain
of kids playing rattlesnake, near the end

when the singing gets frantic, they're jumping, chanting,
eyes shut, shouting. Marie is shouting. We can't move
forward, back to the entrance

where the beautiful young man frisked us for Ecstasy.
We stop at a purple circle, a nervous halo
shaking on the floor. I can't see

eyes. Only teeth. I'm scared,
Marie shouts. Just dance, I motion.
White T-shirts writhe in the dark

like those cartoon ghosts that whoosh across a room,
the shirt moving when the body is gone, sucked
of desire. It's so loud our hearts hurt, but there's nothing

to follow. Someone's teeth curve up. Vampire white,
our smiles are frightening. Big in our faces. Hovering
over T-shirts. I am afraid

this is what heaven will be: body-shaped shades
bleached of their sins, the residual drifting
in space without faces. Who cares

how pure the soul is if you can't see
whose it is? If you can't say this
is Aunt Terri pinning up her hair, Jan

leaning forward to listen the way she does,
Judd unlatching his bicycle helmet. Goodness
to goodness, shirt to shirt, we're beyond

recognition. God, the Buddhists say,
is the breath inside the breath, but what is
dancing without seeing, without

flirting, wanting
someone's—anyone's—hand
to reach around, touch me.

# Reading to Marie from Evelyn Underhill's *Mysticism* on the Train from Florence to Spoleto

We were in the introductory matter—*The Awakening*
*of the Self*—where the person emerges from the daily
emergencies, the mind stirs in its dim prison, and the lights

went out, just for a minute, I thought and waited, holding
my book, and I started to feel before I felt it, Marie getting a
    little
edgy. It's the tunnel, I said, but it was a long time. I put the
    book down and time

stretched out the way it does
when you're on a subway, say, you look up from your book,
your griefs, and think you've missed your stop, you've gone a
    long way

past your station, you're lost, in a dangerous neighborhood,
    can't see
where you are, speeding into a terrible place, then the train
slows and yours is the next stop. But the lights stay out

a long time, longer than that
time I watched the oxygen—days it seemed—condense, dis-
    perse

on Michael's mask—weird precipitation—trying to know
     where he was going.


Trying to tell him. But that's another story. We had taken
one another's hands. We were leaning forward, toward
one another. It made no difference


whether my eyes were open or closed—it was *that* dark
where people faint, where Dante passes out beside Virgil,
where Jane Eyre looks into the mirror and has her famous fit.


But I liked it. There was no telling
how long it would last. And I don't remember myself
and don't want to ask the sequence, but suddenly the lights


came back on, Marie and I leaning toward one another,
holding hands and sunflowers, fields of them,
pressed away together toward some other light


out the windows on one side and the air altered
the sky, clouds groping weird, dark
clouds in the mountains and though it was the hottest middle


of the summer, gathering along the tracks
on the other side—
hail.

# It Happens

One day you're waiting
for the subway, squinting down the coiling
dark, thinking don't cry, don't

start *that* again—thinking
of things like hair, then
*his* hair, thick and gray,

silver, you called it,
*steady and certain as the silver in his hair,*
you wrote once. It was a bad line. Unsteady,

unseasonably bundled, a young
woman stumbles at the edge
of the platform, steps toward the tunnel,

*love, love, love,* she mutters. The subway doesn't
come and still you are thinking
of bike rides, Italian skies,

and you would die to be back—
even in the difficult times.
You never know what you have

until you've lost it. That's what your mother said.
Over and over. She'd lost
her mother, hadn't known—*blah blah*.

The crowd agitates the platform,
*love, love, love*—you are close
to the edge, the train

isn't coming. You balance your
bags, your books, and
read—something, anything. Then light

starts around the bend, the train
approaches and just
when you think you forgot for a second

where you were going,
you see him, that familiar head, his silver hair.
It's what people must feel when they've been held at gun-
        point

about to be robbed, or worse, then last
minute the cops arrive. Or someone. The neighbor.
Like in the movies, when the heroine, at the last moment

decides she's been wrong. She's going back.
But it's not him. You're being shoved
into the car, hugged

up against a stranger in brown tweed,
just like he has, only its not him, the hair
not his, the tweed and you are

rocketing home. You
lean a little
into this stranger's back.

## Ne Me Quitte Pas

The worse I felt, the less
I watered it, the pink
geranium I ignored

all summer. I'd forget
Zoloft, vitamins, the eight
glasses of water I'd commit

each morning to drink.
The dirt went dry, drier on my fire
escape—the leaves

shriveled, the buds withered.
I left the unloved
stumps, refused

to pinch off the neglected
leaves. Now, this morning
insistent, stubborn,

reaching out against ignorance
it cries its furious pink
survival. One single flower.

What makes us hurt what we love?
A man in the window opposite
smokes his cigarette, I smoke

mine, ready to fall
in love, another
beautiful story.

He talks into his cell.
I talk into mine.
Perhaps he's been cruel to a woman,

told her he loved her, took it back.
Perhaps he's been hurt by a lack
of attention, has his mother's eyes.

He strokes his cat. I turn.
Such a wide gulf. Love
left me in the stiff cry of this difficult song.

*Ne me quitte pas,* I sing,
the man no longer there. I turn
drink a glass of water, another,

and another.

# NOTES

*p. 30*   The title of this poem, "The World Gains Luster as It Falls Apart," is taken from Mark Doty's poem "Two Ruined Boats," in *Atlantis* (HarperPerennial 1995).

CPSIA information can be obtained
at www.ICGtesting.com
Printed in the USA
BVOW08s0922271017
498822BV00001B/97/P